GROWING A THRIVING HOPE:

Eternity & Endurance

Essays that Inspire Awe, Joy, and Depth

BY

Jake Daghe

Cover and Interior design by Katie Tynes Watford.
Cover and Interior Typefaces: IM FELL Double Pica and Sorts Mill Goudy

Published by Jake Daghe
Westfield, Indiana

For further information, contact Jake Daghe at jakedaghe.com

Printed in the United States of America
First Edition

ISBN: 979-8-9943421-1-4

"When I think of Jake, I'm reminded of a quote by Andy Crouch, 'Power is for flourishing. Who is flourishing because you have power?' Jake's life embodies this truth. Everything he does is centered on helping others grow in their knowledge, understanding, and awe of Jesus. He uses his power, authority, and leadership not for himself, but to ensure that those around him can truly flourish in their faith."

LEIGHTON CHING, *Creative Director, Passion City Church*

"Jake has been a trusted partner in theology, discipleship, and strengthening the church for years. His commitment to truth, compassion for people, and devotion in ministry are evident in his writing, but more importantly, his life and work."

KAITLIN FEBLES, *Principal Category Lead at Chick-fil-A, Inc. & Writer*

"From heart to hand and pen to page, every word Jake writes effortlessly flows from his ever-flowing love of God, God's people, and God's Kingdom. Growing a Thriving Hope is less of a manual for maturity and more of a living invitation to behold God with renewed awe and joy. Jake's rare union of a theologian's mind and a pastor's heart, alongside His heart for people to flourish in their faith, cultivates nothing short of a masterpiece. Well done, brother!"

ANA HOLT, *Executive Assistant, Passion & Editor, Passion Publishing*

"Few friends have been as formative to my faith as Jake. That's largely thanks to how much he treasures Scripture, hopes for heaven, and thinks deeply about matters worth our attention. Jake's faithfulness to Jesus and fervor for distilling theology give his words a weight worth your time."

LUKE BAKER, *Writer*

Books by Jake Daghe

Growing a Thriving Hope: Reverence & Delight
Growing a Thriving Hope: Eternity & Endurance
Growing a Thriving Hope: Maturity & Pruning

For Grandma Cole -

*until that day when we can revel together
once more in God's unimaginable attributes.*

For Luke -
*for being a constant source of strength,
inspiration, and rich friendship.*

Contents

*"And the Lord will guide you continually
and satisfy your desire in scorched places
and make your bones strong;
and you shall be like a watered garden,
like a spring of water, whose waters do not fail."*

Isaiah 58:11

"I am no man, young or old! I am a boy! Just a boy!"

J.M. Barrie's Peter Pan

*"When the world wearies, and society fails to satisfy,
there is always the garden."*

Minnie Aumonier

Growing a Thriving Hope

A little over five years ago, I came across a quote by the artist and poet Maya Angelou that absolutely shifted something in my soul. At the time, I was approaching my late twenties, and my wife and I were beginning to talk more seriously about having kids. As most do in such moments, I was picking my head up and taking inventory of my life. I was asking big questions that never really have concrete answers. Am I prepared? Is this the right next step for us? Can we do this, and more than that, can we do it well?

Amid this evaluation, I came across this quote, and it honestly changed my perspective in that season. It has stuck with me throughout the highs and lows that have come since. Using her poetic wisdom and way with words, Maya Angelou cut right to the heart of a tension I had felt rising but didn't have the words to name.

She wrote:

> "I am convinced that most people do not grow up. We find parking spaces and honor our credit cards. We marry and dare to

have children and call that growing up. I think what we do is mostly grow old."

I think what we do is mostly *grow old.*

Up until this time, I don't believe I had truly understood the difference between growing up and growing old. And it floored me. As I looked around, I noticed that it wasn't just me wrestling with this tension. All kinds of people were growing old but struggling to figure out how to grow up.

I found myself wanting to know more about these rare people who were truly growing up. Who were becoming more mature. These were the people I started to be drawn to. The ones who seemed confident in who God had made them to be and who seemed to know what peace was. The ones who had fought the battle of putting the self to death and who had come out the other side scarred but victorious. These were the ones I wanted to emulate, the ones I admired.

But I didn't know what it meant to truly grow up. Maya Angelou was right; our society at large confers the status of "grown-up" to those who pass certain age markers — moving out of the house, finishing school, getting married, getting a full-time job. In the eyes of the world, there are many, many grown-ups, but when you really think about it... are there?

For as long as I can remember, I have been moved by the passage in Ephesians 4:11-16. It says,

> "And he gave the apostles, the prophets, the evangelists, the shepherds and teachers, 12 to equip the saints for the work of ministry, for building up the body of Christ, 13 *until we all attain to the unity of the faith and of the knowledge of the Son of God, to mature manhood,*

to the measure of the stature of the fullness of Christ, 14 so that we may no longer be children, tossed to and fro by the waves and carried about by every wind of doctrine, by human cunning, by craftiness in deceitful schemes. 15 Rather, speaking the truth in love, *we are to grow up in every way into him who is the head, into Christ,* 16 from whom the whole body, joined and held together by every joint with which it is equipped, when each part is working properly, makes the body grow so that it builds itself up in love."

Around this time, I began seeing correlations from this text to others, such as 1 Corinthians 13:9-11, which says,

"For we know in part and we prophesy in part, 10 but when the perfect comes, the partial will pass away. 11 When I was a child, I spoke like a child, I thought like a child, I reasoned like a child. *When I became a man, I gave up childish ways.*"

Or 1 John 2:12-13, which says,

"I am writing to you, little children,
     because your sins are forgiven for his name's sake.
13 I am writing to you, *fathers,*
     because you know him who is from the beginning,
I am writing to you, young men,
     because you have overcome the evil one."

Or Hebrews 5:11-14, which says,

"About this we have much to say, and it is hard to explain, since you have become dull of hearing. 12 For though by this time you ought to be teachers, you need someone to teach you again the basic principles of the oracles of God. You need milk, not solid food, 13 for everyone who lives on milk is unskilled in the word of righteousness, since he is a *child.* 14 *But solid food is for the mature,* for those who have their powers of discernment trained by constant practice to distinguish good from evil."

These verses and others, woven together, began to illuminate for me a foundational truth of what it means to be a believer in Christ: that while we are born again by faith into a new life (Jn. 3, Eph. 2), we are meant to then continue to grow up, aiming to become more mature as we conform to the image and likeness of Christ (Rom. 8). This is the process by which we are being transformed, or changed, from one degree of glory to another (2 Cor. 3). Therefore, the objective of the Christian life is to grow up into Christ and to become like him.

This isn't a works-based gospel. It's a fruit-blooming gospel. It's Paul's and James's arguments combined – that true faith is by grace alone, but that faith also must grow and bear fruit as it is connected to the vine. Works only and no works are both symptoms of a dead faith.

Something about this Maya Angelou quote and these Scriptures opened my eyes to this startling reality: I needed help growing up in my faith, not just growing old. I didn't want to have a Peter Pan type of faith where I refused to grow up but just stayed a boy; I wanted to have a deep, rich, mature walk with the Lord that was rooted, like an oak of righteousness.

After I read this quote back in 2020, I spent the next few years practicing this pursuit while also thinking about how to help others pursue a deeper, more mature faith. Over that time and through many conversations, this image of comparing our faith to a garden began to take shape in my mind and heart. I began using the language of "*Growing a Thriving Hope*" to describe the process of cultivating a vibrant, strong faith.

During the pandemic years, my wife and I, like many others, got more into gardening. It was largely fun... for a while (minus the constant watering in the early days after planting). We loved seeing the plants grow, and months later, we were awed by the small but significant harvest we reaped. We were amateurs in every meaning of the word, which suited us just fine. But it didn't necessarily suit our garden long-term. Pests got in, our supports got broken after a few years of use, and we struggled to keep systems in place that led to good soil and good harvests. The costs were relatively high, and while we still planted a garden the following years, our expectations and effort tended to drop year over year.

Does that sound familiar? In many ways, I could be describing most of our faith journeys. Things might start out great and seem to really take off, but over time, the consistent grind of maintenance and growth just wears us down. We don't abandon our faith so much as we just settle into a half-hearted practice. Just like a garden, without good focus, the right tools, and hard work, our harvest starts to dwindle. Our garden of faith just keeps growing older, but it doesn't actually grow up into a richer, fuller, more vibrant, and healthier expression of maturity.

This is the primary reason I wrote this series of essays. I wanted to explore topics that I believe are very significant to our faith but might be presently overlooked or underexplored. And I wanted to write about these subjects in a format that mirrored the ideal outcome with rich, mature, weighty words. I don't mind that these essays are somewhat dense or that they're best read slowly. Maturity is a slow process.

I truly do believe that if you are looking to grow up in your faith, or if you are looking to answer that question: what's next for me in my walk with Jesus? this series of essays is a great place to start cultivating your soul's garden as you look to see your hope and faith thrive again.

As I was finishing up these manuscripts, I came across this verse in Isaiah 58:11, which perfectly matched the vision of what I was trying to accomplish. It reads,

> "And the Lord will guide you continually and satisfy your desire in scorched places and make your bones strong; and you shall be like a watered garden, like a spring of water, whose waters do not fail."

I trust that you and I can see the Lord guide us as he makes us to be like a watered garden. We can once more be like a spring whose waters do not fail. We can see our hope thrive, and when it does, we will see faith bloom anew in our hearts as we eagerly long for the beautiful fruits unique to the Christian faith. We can see the soil of our souls fortified, preparing the way so that we grow up into Jesus, not just grow old around him.

As you get ready to dig into this work, I'd like to offer a short prayer that God would grant you a healthy ambition for maturity.

Lord, I pray that we, together, would walk wisely with an increasing passion for your name. We are aware that it is possible, even easy, to pursue conforming to Christ from the wrong motivations or for the wrong outcomes. But Spirit, help us and keep us focused, guard our hearts and minds, that as we aim ourselves towards your eternal glory, you would empower and equip us with all that we need for a life of godliness. Would you enlighten the eyes of our hearts that we would know what is the hope that we have been called to; that we would behold the riches of your glorious inheritance in the saints and the immeasurable greatness of your power toward us who believe. May we seek to offer acceptable and true worship, and may we eagerly yearn for that coming day when the final victory is established, sin is banished, and our souls will see the Person whom we have come to love and adore.

Lord, make it so. Move us out of our comforts and propel us into a passionate pursuit of you. Wake us up, Lord, and give us the grace we need to grow a thriving hope.

Under the roar of heaven,

Jake

*"The work of the Christian is not to win quickly,
but to remain faithful."*

HENRI NOUWEN

"We live in time, but we are shaped for forever."

GEORGE MACDONALD

Eternity & Endurance

Few things have impacted my life and faith more than reflecting and dwelling on the idea of eternity. I long for the things of heaven, not so much materialistically, but metamorphically; the essence and transformation of glory's redeeming power over all that we know and see today. I am convinced beyond a shadow of a doubt that whatever we can imagine heaven to be, it will be infinitely greater. We, in this time, cannot begin to comprehend the nuance and nature of a resurrected and redeemed creation.

God says in Revelation 21:5, "Behold, I am making all things new." Whether we realize it or not, this is our heart's greatest hope: that rather than spend the rest of our lives fighting these same struggles and these same battles, there will come a day when *everything* will be made new. Not just our physical bodies, although praise God for no more sickness that lingers or ailment that weighs us down. Resurrection is a very physical reality, but there is so much more to resurrection than simply having breath re-enter our lungs. As we are resurrected, our nerve endings become re-awakened, if that is an appropriate thought for this element of redemption. We are suddenly able to feel again, but now we will do so in a resurrected and righteous way. Every sensation of our bodies will be glory, every smell, every sight, every touch, every sound, every taste. No longer will we see something and desire it in a way that exchanges that value with our value of God. Our eyes will never again make idols of what we see, but we will always see the world around us rightly ordered with God's glory as our ultimate value.

No longer will we hear a single word that tempts our hearts to turn from God and to lean on our own devices, our own strength, or our own judgments. Imagine that! We will hear perfectly, so as to always give and receive through word or sound that which is most worshipful to the Father. We will not hear frustration, for there will be no means for that which is frustrating to interfere with our perpetual praise. We will not hear or partake in complaint or grumbling, we will not hear slander or devaluing speech. We will only hear that which elevates our hearts to worship. This does not mean that we will speak only in holy hymnal, but that our everyday, regular speech will be so perfected and glorious that it cannot detract from our exaltation in the slightest.

Our hands will never again abuse power, never again feel in the dark what we would not touch in the light, for all is light, and all is holy. We will never make another thing for our own glory or our own image. We will craft, work, build... not to repair but to revel in the reality of resurrection, as our hands will be perfect in their doing. We will not work to compete in the way that we currently understand competition, but rather, we will work in conjunction with our neighbor, because there will be no sense of elevation or humiliation at the expense of another. There will be only wonder, only offering our very selves as worship because every moment we do will be delightful to and delighting in God Almighty.

None of this is as restrictive as we were led to believe in our youth. I am increasingly stunned at the brashness of Satan, who has somehow convinced a large portion of Christians that heaven will be tame, mild-mannered, and even boring or uneventful. Imagine the gall of the deceiver to take that which will be the most lively, the most joyous, the most holy and wondrous reality, and to dilute it to such a level that we could somehow conclude that heaven will be stuffy and restricting in its rule of worship.

Will we worship? Yes! In an infinite number of expressions that reflect the resurrected and redeemed creation of our great and holy God. If that idea of worship seems lackluster, our hearts may not truly grasp the reality of wanting God more than any earthly treasure.

Eternity will be many things, but it will never be boring. That which is most satisfying can never be unappealing to those who are truly longing to be satisfied.

When we consider the wonder of eternity that truly awaits just beyond this vapor of a life, our hearts are established in hope. We are founded in joy as we lift our heads and look toward that quickly approaching reality. It is only here, only with this hope as our guide, that we can properly and patiently endure any and all trials in this current age.

Endurance is a hard task for our hearts to grasp because it seems like an unnecessary burden for those who serve an all-powerful God. As the popular refrain goes, if God is loving and all-powerful, why does suffering exist? Said another way, why is endurance an aspect of the Christian life? Couldn't God just remove all of our discomfort and difficulty?

This introduction is not the place to delve into the full apologetic on the problem of evil, but I will say this in short order: the world is broken by sin. Some hardship stems from our personal sin, some from others' sin, and some yet stems from the broken systems and structures of our world. Rather than eradicate sin now, which would result in many not being saved, God, in his mercy, delays his final judgment. In doing so, he allows his saints to walk through the hardship of a world that is eagerly groaning for redemption. As we walk, we too yearn more truly for that eternal reward that is shortly coming.

This worshipful yearning, this heavy holiness, can witness to the broken world that there is something available that is greater than any treasure the world can offer. God uses hardship to redeem, refine, and re-awaken a sleeping world to the reality of His resurrection.

We will not always enjoy this process, and we certainly won't always approve of the ways God works. Our approval was never part of the requirement for God's actions. Which means that we can still worship in whatever darkness we find ourselves in on Earth. When we know that eternity waits just around the corner, we can rise once more to our feet, lift our hands, and echo the words of Job in chapter 1, verse 21:

"And he said, "Naked I came from my mother's womb, and naked shall I return. The Lord gave, and the Lord has taken away; blessed be the name of the Lord.""

These two – eternity and endurance – must go hand in hand. There is little point, beyond pure obedience, in enduring if eternity is not significantly greater than our imaginations. Likewise, there is no need for an eternity that is far greater than today if today were optimally satisfying. Do you see the relationship? We endure because eternity is before us, but eternity must be before us because there is cause to endure today. We will never be satisfied on this side of heaven, but there will be a day when we will be perfectly satisfied.

That is the hope of this pair of essays: to lift our eyes to the Light of the coming dawn, and to levitate our hearts above the fray of the hardship here and now.

*"But as it is, they desire a better country,
that is, a heavenly one. Therefore God is
not ashamed to be called their God,
for he has prepared for them a city."*

HEBREWS 11:16

*"...according to his great mercy, he has caused
us to be born again to a living hope through the
resurrection of Jesus Christ from the dead, ⁴to an
inheritance that is imperishable, undefiled, and
unfading, kept in heaven for you, ⁵who by God's
power are being guarded through faith for a
salvation ready to be revealed in the last time."*

1 PETER 1:3-5

ESSAY I

Eternity

My fellow futurists,

It is common knowledge that many believers, not to mention most nonbelievers, have concerns about the future and how certain challenges, hardships, or unknowns will unfold. In some ways, this feels like a rite of passage for being a human being. We are prone to looking uneasily into those murky waters of tomorrow, hoping to glean a sliver of understanding or peace for the days ahead. To be clear, it is not necessarily sinful to show concern for tomorrow; in fact, there can be much wisdom in thoughtful concern and considerate preparation for the days ahead. But more often than not, our concern can quickly shift into obsession and a fixation on the future.

We say we want a clear path, a well-drawn blueprint of what lies ahead, but what we are really after in those moments of future longing is, at its root, control. We want to know when and how our lives will unfold so we can prepare in ways that align with our self-sufficiency, thereby eliminating any dependence on others. We want to live as our own mini-kings and queens, and we've become convinced that knowing all the answers regarding life's plan is a sure step toward claiming that ruling throne.

Simply because there can be a dangerous[1] and devious connection between future longing and future fixation, does that mean that we, as believers, should aim instead to never think of the days to come? It seems that popular culture and even the Church largely agree with this train of thought: that it is better to err on the side of being completely present-minded as an attempt to fight future-mindedness.

However, I believe we do ourselves a disservice when we avoid looking ahead and instead, commit to looking only at our feet and the next step in front of us. Within each of us, there is a desire — a longing for the future — I'd venture should not be quickly disregarded or fiercely squashed. In fact, rather than condemning this future fixation, we should, by the power of the Spirit of God, seek to strengthen this desire, making it a pivotal component of our daily Christian life and practice.

It is important to note that I am not advocating for a future fixation that can be achieved, or satisfied, in this life or world. Although this desire for the future is written on our hearts and pressed into our souls,[2] we have often erred in how we

---

1. Like the lotus eaters of Homer's *The Odyssey*, living in the future can be akin to a tantalizing dream of bliss and self-control, one in which the dreamer never wants to leave or stop.

2. Ecclesiastes 3:11 says that God has put eternity into the hearts of man.

apply these desires. We have chosen, unwisely, to place the execution or recognition of these longings within the framework of earthly realities and not spiritual ones. We have too easily taken the lesser treat to satiate our hunger when the 5-star, full-course meal is just about to leave the kitchen.

For those who are anxious or overwhelmed with thoughts about the future, I do not think future fixation is the primary problem. Rather, our anxiety and sense of overwhelm likely stem from the rather sneaky temptation to fixate on the wrong iteration of the future. Let me clarify.

If you are in Christ, you have before you only one future, but it is bifurcated by your physical death and physical resurrection into eternal life. If we take that bifurcation as a dividing line, we can categorize everything from now until your physical death as "future-earth." And we can categorize everything from your physical resurrection onward as "future-eternity."[3]

Too often, we spend our lives trying to guess, manipulate, and perfect future-earth while we allow the truths and beauties of future-eternity to be underappreciated or, worse, unexplored.

This is our central tension: we have a longing, a tangible desire, for future realities. We want to know what comes next.

---

3. I understand that some would argue that all of life post-conversion is future-eternity, but I am attempting to recognize the final distinction of the believer: our life now until we physically die where we are still battling the flesh, and our life after our death and resurrection where we are perfectly glorified and redeemed.

Yet, if we are not careful and intentional, we will spend our short lives satiating our future longing by attempting to control the unknowns of future-earth. But as we know all too well, this world, and this life, is ultimately beyond our control.

Instead, we should fix our eyes and minds on the certain and fulfilling truths of future-eternity. Though we may not understand the exact application of future-eternity, what we do know for sure should be enough to fuel our endurance, stabilize our hope, and anchor our faith.

Now, it is not wrong to pray and seek clarity for all that lies ahead on future-earth. In fact, we are invited to turn to God in the haze of the unknown. Petitions to God for strength, clarity, and grace are not to be frowned upon simply because there is a clear and coming future reality of eternal life with Christ.

Though both sin and death have been defeated by the cross and resurrection of Christ, they have not yet been vanquished. Resurrection and new life are the real and known realities of the future coming time; however, the creation today is still "groaning in the pains of childbirth."[4] We still face everyday decisions and unknowns that we must approach with faith, hope, and endurance.

Therefore, it is wise to be prayerfully intentional with what we have been entrusted with in future-earth. We should desire to steward well our marriages, our jobs, our homes, our investments, our children, our gifts, our skills, and our talents. We want to be like the good and faithful servants

---

4. Romans 8:22

who, when handed a certain measure of trust, e.g., talents,[5] invested those talents and put them to "good use." That is the basis of the reward in the parable, what the servants did in the days of future-earth with what they had been given.

While we seek God for the short-term, we are encouraged in the Scripture to also look further ahead to the long-term, the coming reality of future-eternity. It is here that we can find true certainty that sustains our souls. It would be a great shame to neglect the most beautiful bedrock of assurance available to the believer: eternity.

In this vein, I'm reminded of the opening verses of the Apostle Peter's first letter to the elect exiles of the Dispersion. As a brief aside, I find it particularly encouraging that these letters are written to exiles, given that according to the writer of Hebrews, that is exactly what you and I are in our present day: strangers and aliens of both this present and future-earth. For those of us who are in Christ, we are true citizens of a coming city, an eternal destination and home. And so, in writing to the elect exiles, Peter reminds them that according to God's great mercy, which is worked out through the blood and sacrifice of Christ, we have been born again to a living hope through the resurrection.

One of the most delightful and soothing certainties stemming from the future-eternity is that you now have a true anchor called hope. We are men and women who long to hope for good things. This is why we love stories of

---

5. A talent is worth 20 years labor / wages. So each talent given to the servants was a huge implication of trust and wealth.

redemption, reconciliation, and overcoming. There is something deep within each of us that wants to hope, but we are often hesitant to fully embrace that desire because our lived experience has taught us that hoping in the uncertainty of future-earth is a risky venture.

Because we live on a broken planet, surrounded by broken people, hope does not always triumph, which, therefore, makes it uncertain. You can hope that your troubles go away tomorrow, but that doesn't mean that they will. You can hope that you won't have money problems in the days ahead, that your health will remain strong and unwavering, that your parenting will be successful, or that your dreams will be fulfilled, but none of those things are guaranteed. They aren't even "likely" to all come to fruition. You do not need a long explanation to grasp that earthly hope is frequently battered and bruised by the uncontrollable and occasionally devastating realities of our life here on Earth.

But pause and rejoice with me over the certainties of that greater and more glorious future reality. Future-eternity is no future-earth, starting with the truth that the outcomes of our God-aligned desires are fully guaranteed. There will be no more sickness. No more sorrow. No more pain or uncontrollable circumstances. All will be joy. All will be pure. All will be bright, with no shadows from the risk of things changing or being swept away.

This is a future worth hoping for. There is no instability, but rather an inevitability of good that can spur confidence; an assurance that stakes our hope like a tent peg being driven into the soft soil. The Apostle Peter calls this a "living hope" because that which is spiritually alive (especially eternally) is no longer subject to the pangs and stings of death or decay.

Can you begin to taste that future certainty? This is what Hebrews 6 refers to: "*We have this as a sure and steadfast anchor of the soul, a hope that enters into the inner place behind the curtain.*" This living hope is Christ, who, when he became a man, took on the form of humanity, putting himself likewise in the position of having his future bifurcated by a pending death.

However, death was not the end for Jesus. As we know, he resurrected and then ascended to the right hand of the Father, thus establishing for us the assurance of our future-eternity; the basis of our confidence. Christ, now sitting in the throne room of God, personally guarantees both our righteousness and our right standing. His presence in heaven provides the clarity for our future reality. Since he is the hope that has entered the inner place, and because he is alive forevermore, we can be confident that such a hope is sure and steadfast.

Do you see the distinction between the two future realities? If I asked you to predict your future, you would have no basis for confidence, because all your attempts to forecast your days rely on your intuition and your understanding of how things will unfold. And as Jesus so bluntly shared with his disciples in Matthew 6, why do we think we are wise or strong enough to make accurate predictions when we cannot even do something as simple as add a single hour to our lifespans? We are not even guaranteed our next day, our next hour, or our next breath. We can no more demand sure and steadfast clarity of our days on future-earth than we can attempt to hold the ocean in our hands.

However, if I asked you to predict your future-eternity, now there would be an answer! Once you start sharing, you may not be able to stop. What a blessed guarantee of a victorious hope in Christ!

Returning to chapter 1 of Peter's first letter to the elect exiles, look at what comes after this living hope. As if that were not enough, we are also set to receive an inheritance, which Peter describes in verses 4-5. He writes that we will receive "an inheritance that is imperishable, undefiled, and unfading, kept in heaven for you, who by God's power are being guarded through faith for a salvation ready to be revealed in the last time."

These verses always make my breath hitch in my chest as I realize, once again, how magnificent and marvelous God is. How abundant and generous he is towards us, his children. Don't pass over these words too quickly. We have a guaranteed *inheritance* awaiting us in the future-eternity.

I believe that our eternal inheritance will include more than our permanent right-standing in Christ. I hope it is very clear, however, that I also believe that anything additional that we attain beyond Christ will be of secondary importance or worthiness compared to that received and imputed righteousness.

I believe that our future-eternity will consist of a physical environment to be lived out on a new Earth, and therefore, this "inheritance," built upon the cornerstone of Christ's sacrifice, goes on to contain all things pertaining to joy and holy surrender to God.

What that inheritance may be exactly for you, I cannot say, but I do know that heaven is Christ-centric and creation-redeeming, which means that you and I will receive both spiritual and physical treasures. And they will be far greater, richer, and more significant than we can even begin to dare to imagine. If we tried to imagine the beauty of that inheritance, our spirits would faint within us in overwhelming awe before we could scratch the surface of that which awaits us.

It is not of utmost importance to determine what the exact specifications of our eternal inheritance are, but it is essential that we do not underestimate our impending inheritance to the point that we no longer hunger and thirst for that coming day. It is far too easy to look longingly at the seemingly shiny treasures of the future-earth, and in our hearts, hold more affection for these pieces of fool's gold than to properly value and yearn for the real treasure and heft of eternity's glory.

Describing our inheritance to come, Peter uses three stunning words: imperishable, undefiled, and unfading. The implications of each are potent. Imperishable shows us that our inheritance can withstand any attack. It is never dented, scratched, or diminished. It is not threatened by any action or any person. It is immune to devastation, darkness, and even, ultimately, to our own efforts. This word shows us that our inheritance cannot perish, meaning it cannot go away or be reduced. It is maintained perfectly; established. Indestructible. Absolute. Certain.

It is also undefiled, which in its essence means pure. It is the exact fulfillment of beauty and enrichment, that which will most fully satisfy the heart and mind. There are no catches, contracts, or back payments. No gimmicks or too-good-to-be-trues. It is nourishing in every way. We will not get to heaven and ever, even for one microsecond, have the thought that our inheritance is not enough. We will never look at what is stored up for us and think, "I wish I had," in a way that incites lack or envy. Those emotions and corresponding behaviors will have no place in the future-eternity.

Now, without becoming too much of a prophet about things I cannot explain or comprehend, my reading of the Scripture leads me to believe that there can and likely will be different amounts associated with different individual inheritances. But because your inheritance is undefiled, I must suppose that somehow, there will be an element of distinction without comparison. So, if you have more or less than your neighbor, it will not lead to shame or pride, but in either case, you will worship in full as you are able and as the starkly beautiful truth of *who* provided the inheritance overwhelms all other senses.

I know it might seem impractical to spend so much time thinking about a future reality we cannot possibly fully explain. But what is more impractical—to commit to thinking about that great day coming or to live with obliviousness, or worse, denial, because we weren't willing to engage with the mysterious?

Lastly, Peter describes our inheritance as unfading, which I take to mean that it never loses an ounce of glory and beauty. If imperishable describes the fortitude of the inheritance and undefiled describes its purity, then unfading describes its perpetual, infinite, continuous worthiness. There will never be a time when your inheritance is less glorious. Its worthiness is not contingent on any earthly standard or tare. It does not fluctuate like the dollar or the British pound. Our inheritance is not riding the ups and downs of the S&P500. Christ imbues this inheritance with his value, and therefore, it is eternally of the utmost caliber.

These are big concepts to grasp, and it can certainly feel like we have ventured out into the deep end of the pool. And yet, it is important to dwell on such rich truths, especially regarding what is to come, because it helps bring perspective to the uncertainties and struggles found in both the current and future-earth domains.

We are all looking for something to assure us that our lives count for or toward something. Otherwise, why do we live? Why do we strive? Why do we fight back against the hard and dark circumstances around us? The main difference, then, between future-earth and future-eternity is that in future-earth, our efforts are the primary metric for addressing this tension. Thus, we control our significance and worth through our contribution. Whereas in future-eternity, Jesus' actions have already established an infinitely worthy inheritance.

Tim Keller once wrote that Christianity is the only religion where the verdict is delivered before the performance. If future-earth is defined by our performance, then future-eternity is defined by God's verdict over our lives: forgiven, free, adopted, redeemed, and co-heirs with Jesus.

We no longer must strive to be strong enough to withstand all the unknowns that will inevitably crop up in future-earth. We no longer have to be "good enough," through our own merit, to earn our salvation and to warrant self-righteousness. When we over-fixate on future-earth, we are hyperinflating our own value and importance in the story — that somewhere in the unknown sea of days to come lies a moment where we will have aligned every detail to a reasonable level of perfection so that we can be worthy of a future inheritance.

But that is not the gospel, and that is not the way to truly live free today. Rather, when we live with our minds fueled and fixated on the eternal treasure so graciously provided by Christ, when we see that future-eternity as the foundation for our faith and the source of a sure and steadfast hope that will never let us down, never fail, never diminish, then we have the ultimate answer that unlocks every struggle, tension, and unmet desire in our earthly lives, today and to come.

How do we have confident hope rather than wavering hope? By longing for the future-eternity. How do we have peace amidst the chaos, confidence in the uncertainty, strength in the struggle, joy in the suffering, bravery in the danger, stability in the precariousness? How do we have faith in the darkness of a sin-stained world? By fixing our eyes on Christ, our future-eternity, and on our heavenly inheritance to come.

As I conclude this essay, I want to turn your attention to Hebrews 11. Specifically, I want us to linger on a few verses in this familiar chapter.

Hebrews 11 is often called the "Hall of Faith" because this chapter includes a magnificent list of men and women who followed God and walked in accordance with his promises and ways. But tucked between these short descriptions are some powerful verses around this idea of future-eternity.

In the description of Abraham, one line in particular stands out to me: *"For he was looking forward to the city that has foundations, whose designer and builder is God."*

In the cultural context of Abraham's day, a fortified or well-founded city was the epitome of strength, power, and protection. Abraham, in following God's promise, was sent from his homeland to become a wanderer, one without a secure city or shelter to call home. So, Abraham would have been fully justified in longing for a city with strong foundations. But we see that rather than dwell on that desire coming to fruition in future-earth, Abraham was looking forward (i.e., future-eternity minded) to the city whose designer and builder is God (i.e., the coming inheritance, or a portion thereof).

Later in Hebrews 11, we see more language about this future city in verses 13-16:

> These all died in faith, not having received the things promised, but having seen them and greeted them from afar, and having acknowledged that they were strangers and exiles on the earth. For people who speak thus make it clear that they are seeking a homeland.

> If they had been thinking of that land from which they had gone out, they would have had opportunity to return. But as it is, they desire a better country, that is, a heavenly one. Therefore God is not ashamed to be called their God, for he has prepared for them a city.

There is much to take heart at in these few verses. First, notice that even the greatest in our lineage of faith did not receive the fullness of their promised inheritance in the future-earth. Because of the infestation of sin, it is actually impossible to receive the fullness of our eternal inheritance here and now. But though they did not receive what was promised, this did not stop them from seeing and greeting those promises from afar.

This is the crux of this essay: are you actively seeing *and* greeting your future inheritance? You do not need to go about your life staring at your feet, putting all your effort into living a present-minded life devoid of any future-longing or fixation. Rather, consider this simple question: are your eyes rightly valuing what is to come in heaven more than what is to come on Earth? And when your eyes do see the distinction, how is that difference driving your behavior and beliefs? Are you grumbling about the uncontrollable nature of your future-earth, or are you greeting your future-eternity, merrily acknowledging and welcoming its approach?

This greeting does not stop us from acknowledging our present realities. On this Earth, there will be difficulty and decay. We can grieve the tensions of being strangers and exiles. But in our grief and our struggle, we can look up and glimpse the ever-approaching reality of our heavenly home.

Our joyous and hopeful greeting of future-eternity can shift something within us. We can start to think like those who have an assured inheritance. We can begin to talk like those who are heirs, like those who are expectant of a sure and coming victory.

If we think and speak primarily of future-earth, we will find, similar to the Pharisees in Jesus' day, that we will get our reward in full, here and now. But if we long for and look to that future treasure in eternity, if we desire with our whole beings that coming city, then we will find that we are confident and at peace in our remaining days on Earth.

Lastly, look at Hebrews 11:25, a short but powerful description of Moses. It reads: *"He considered the reproach of Christ greater wealth than the treasures of Egypt, for he was looking to the reward."*

What a beautiful thread woven throughout these texts! What an invitation to you and me today to *look forward*, to look to the coming reward, and to rightly value that treasure over any and all that might threaten to steal our attention. It takes a unique effort to continually shift the attraction of our hearts from future-earth to future-eternity. I pray that you are encouraged to believe the effort is worth it. Jesus is empowering you and drawing you to himself.

The light of heaven will one day reveal that every other light is merely a reflection. When it does, I desperately hope that you can celebrate that you aimed your whole life at the true and proper light.

Longing with you for that eternal joy,

J. Daghe

1.

What role does future fixation play in your story right now? Are you constantly being tugged to think about the future, or are you more focused on being present-minded? How could a better understanding of your future-eternity help you find peace in your future-earth?

2.

What about eternity is most exciting and appealing to you? Why does this captivate your heart?

Lord, open the eyes of our hearts that we may see with greater clarity those truths of resurrection and redemption that are just over the horizon. Root our faith in that coming joy that we may be at peace, whatever may come during our days here.

Interlude

When I set out to write books of paired essays, I knew I wanted to connect eternity to endurance. These two concepts are significantly intertwined, as I believe we endure in large part because we truly believe in and hope for an eternity that is perfectly fulfilling and good.

Endurance is the essay I rewrote the most, as I really wrestled with walking the fine line of seeing suffering as a necessity of the Christian faith without idolizing our hardship.

Far too many Christians either chase after sufferings as a type of merit badge to be gained or tuck their coattails between their legs and flee from any type of hardship. We are prone to prioritize the pride that comes from our scars or the comforts that come from a life devoid of calluses. So, as I wrote and rewrote this essay, I wrestled with trying to capture this tension in a way that speaks to what I believe is the biblical reality: in this world, we will have troubles. We will suffer, whether from the natural brokenness of this world, the consequences of our own sin and struggle, or the evil perpetrated against us by all varieties of people and principalities.

Therefore, those who call Christ Lord, being mindful of this reality, must prioritize the discipline of endurance, of lasting, not grumpily or with a manner of resignation. For where is the witness in that? If we truly believe in the eternity to come, that the most beautiful, most spectacular, most redemptive, most holy, most joyous, most satisfying future is just over the next horizon, then why would we let anything here and now outweigh or dampen that quickly approaching celebration?

No, we must endure hopefully and joyfully; two words that are difficult to pair with endurance, especially in a self-centered, eye-for-an-eye world. But we are not of this world if eternity is our true destination. That truth must shape how we interact with hardship today, and therefore, when we fixate on future-eternity, we are emboldened, almost enlivened, to endure well here and now!

After all, is there possibly a better witness than someone who is so convinced of a joy to come that they are willing to withstand losses, however significant, and remain upright, kind, and joyful? This does not discount grief, or mourning, or dealing with very real emotions and despair. But it does mean that our endurance is bigger than a simple "tough-it-out" mentality. It is connected to our future-eternity, and if that future is good, then we can live content today, regardless of what comes our way.

*"Not only that, but we rejoice in our sufferings,
knowing that suffering produces endurance,
⁴and endurance produces character, and character
produces hope, ⁵and hope does not put us to shame,
because God's love has been poured into our hearts
through the Holy Spirit who has been given to us."*

Romans 5:3-5

Endurance

To those who are looking for hope,

Staying faithful and maintaining a steady pursuit of Christ amid a harrowing season may seem illogical or near impossible. You may even begin to feel like there is no merit in carrying on, in trying to stay steady, or in trusting in God's goodness. If you have found yourself, or currently find yourself, at the bottom of the hill of hardship, the last words your heart may want to hear are: keep enduring.

I understand that these words might seem like I am suggesting using a Band-Aid to cover up a bullet hole. Hardship can be heavy, messy, and disillusioning. I have personally felt the bitter tendrils of suffering; parts of my story include dreams broken on hospital room floors and personal insecurities from disabilities long suffered. And yet, because I have sat in these shadows, it is not glib when I say that endurance is a source of joy far more brilliant and sustaining than we often realize or give credit to.

Endurance is a way of relating to Christ and to this world that empowers believers and anchors their faith and hope. It is the impetus of character, a confirmation of heavenly citizenship, and one of the central tenets of love.[6]

I'm of the mind, and I hope to gently show, that despite its sourness upon swallowing, endurance may be the best path the believer should aspire to walk. We all will suffer; that is without question, even if we aim to remove all suffering from our lives. Brokenness eventually bites us all. Therefore, this life is not about avoiding suffering as much as it is about responding rightly when suffering enters or remains in our story.

Far greater than either ease (a lack of hardship) or escape (a rejection of hardship), endurance is the essence of the Christian life before eternity and is, in many ways, the pinnacle of maturity for those redeemed by Christ, those who aspire to grow a thriving hope.

Therefore, if you find yourself in times that seem unclear and contemptuous, keep enduring. Even when you feel like you have no other option and nothing is breaking your way, embrace endurance, as it can fundamentally alter how you bear up under your circumstances. Even if you would not consider yourself to be actively suffering, you can still begin to build a helpful and holy framework for endurance that will sustain you when the storms of life do eventually roll your way.

---

6. As per 1 Cor. 13:7 - "Love bears all things, believes all things, hopes all things, endures all things."

When exploring and wrestling with the idea of endurance, it is helpful to begin by defining terms. Therefore, when I use endurance, I think of the word primarily through this lens: *endurance is the faith-fueled action of patiently and joyfully lasting or standing firm through today's hardships in view of a better tomorrow.*

Before stepping into the specifics of how to endure, it is essential to first understand what endurance is and why it is so necessary for believers to embrace and cultivate it in their hearts and minds.

While this definition offers a more comprehensive view of the work of endurance, I also enjoy a shorter definition that draws on a connection between John 16:33 and 2 Corinthians 4:16. The first says,

> "I have said these things to you, that in me you may have peace. In the world you will have tribulation. But take heart; I have overcome the world."

While the second reads,

> "So we do not lose heart. Though our outer self is wasting away, our inner self is being renewed day by day."

In studying the threads that connect these verses, we can summarize that endurance is the *action of taking heart and not losing heart.* It is the work of not giving up, even when it seems like giving up is the most natural or necessary thing to do.

Taking heart and not losing heart is an active decision. Too often, we approach endurance with a form of resigned pessimism. We look at the hardship or difficulty that is threatening to overwhelm us, and we begin to believe that there is nothing more we can or should do than to sit back and bitterly take the blows. We begin to wish that we would simply get through the hardship rather than grow through it or even gain from it.[7]

However, when you commit to taking heart and not losing heart, you shift that narrative. No longer are you resigned to sit in suffering as a victim of your hardship. You are an active agent in fighting for hope. In partnership with the Spirit, you join the spiritual resistance against the darkness. You are taking heart, taking courage, taking a sense of emboldened hope. You are aligning with Christ, surrendering your daily weakness for his heavenly strength. You come to see the hardship you are facing not with a pessimistic sense of gloom but with a focused sense of purpose, that you should fight, last, and stand firm regardless, or in spite of, the circumstance.

Despite longing for an easy path, we are all aware that suffering and hardship are an undeniable reality of being alive on Earth. Pain, sadness, despair, heartbreak, sickness, even death - these are all components of every story.

And yet still, even in the face of such awareness, we deceive ourselves into thinking that if we prepare well, protect ourselves from every angle, or even pray, inducing spiritual assistance, that we can somehow claim exemption

---

7. I know that when difficulty hits, we are often not thinking of "gaining" something as a result of the hardship. Often, we need to do the work of grieving before we ever "gain" anything, but there is a difference in the way we set our minds, as victims of hardship or as children of God who are being formed in the fires of this life.

from the inevitable as we seek to live a happy, suffering-free, smooth path type of life. We must lay aside the meddlesome and clingy ideology that ease, comfort, or happiness devoid of hardship is the epitome of a successful, enjoyable life.

By and large, believers know they are to guard against a "health and wealth" or "prosperity" gospel, in which faith in Jesus is the key that unlocks our every fleshly desire and sense of well-being. And yet, so many believers still subconsciously associate their Christian faith with a guarantee of worldly blessing, heightened materialism, and limited hardship or suffering.

If we are not intentional, faith can begin to feel very much like karma, which is never more evident than when difficulty arises. If you've ever been in that spot, you know how easily the heart can turn slightly aside and begin questioning, "God, what did I do to *deserve* this?"[8]

While that can be a genuine question, understanding the role of hardship in the believer's life helps reframe our approach to the tension of suffering. The Scripture isn't shy in its implication that hardship is a crucial and common component of the Christian walk. In fact, it goes so far as to say that "in this world, we *will* have trouble."[9] It also says that we are to "count it all joy *when* we meet trials of various kinds."[10] Not *if* we meet trials, but *when* we meet trials.

---

8. Most of the time this question is asked, we are inherently assuming that because of our "goodness" or faith-related participation, we are undeserving of difficulty.

9. John 16:33

10. James 1:2

Not only will we actively experience the tensions of living in a broken world – Romans 8 says that the creation is "groaning in the pains of childbirth" – but making the decision to follow Christ and to be associated with him means that we must follow his example and aim to live as he lived.

Reading through the gospels, you see time and time again that Christ endured hardship, and therefore, we should expect to do the same. Why should we expect that our lives would look vastly different from our Lord and Master? This is the basis of 1 Peter 4:1, which says, "Since therefore Christ suffered in the flesh, arm yourselves with the same way of thinking."

In this vein, I believe there are three major categories of hardship that we must be aware of and that every believer should be ready to experience in some way throughout their life. I label these categories as external, internal, and association hardships. These types of hardship may bleed together in some circumstances.

When you can name the avenues by which suffering may enter your story, it allows you to prepare for that hardship. You can begin to identify the root of both your suffering and your response to your suffering. As you do, you can commit to enduring in every category you may face. This will give you the solid foundation to "remain steadfast under trial" per James 1.

The first category to look at is *externally* caused hardship. External suffering is that which happens to you, that which is beyond your control. You can also think of this as passive hardship, meaning that you did not do anything to elicit or invoke this suffering. This is hardship that happens simply because we live in a fallen and broken world.

Think of the difficulties people run up against, things like bodily harm or betrayal. Defamation or theft. Sickness that comes unexpectedly. A pregnancy that may end in loss. A natural disaster that may befall your city. There are dozens of ways that we face struggle and hardship because we exist in a world where things are not as they should be.

The second form of hardship is more internally caused. These hardships come through two primary channels: self-inflicted and self-imposed. The second is uniquely tailored to the Christian.

The first form of internal hardship is self-inflicted. Even those who do not practice faith recognize that there are moral standards and laws that should be obeyed. When we, through our deliberate actions, compromise those standards or break those laws, there are consequences, most of which lead to some form of hardship. These hardships do not erase grace or remove salvation for a believer; they are often just consequences of sinful decisions.

If you choose to pursue an adulterous relationship and are caught, your marriage will likely become fractured, and loss of intimacy may ensue. If you lie about your financial situation or take money that is not yours and get caught, you may face legal consequences and hardship, including punishment or even incarceration. These are self-inflicted hardships, circumstances that result from our own decisions and choices.

Internal suffering can also be self-imposed. This form of hardship should be a daily practice for the believer, and it should result in the fruitfulness of characteristics like joy, peace, patience, and others listed in Galatians 5.

Throughout human history, the world has co-opted self-imposed hardship through means such as self-help, Stoic philosophies, and personal disciplines. These are all tools humanity has leveraged to pursue optimized performance or satisfaction. We have always understood that something seems to be missing, and so we've chased the ideals of betterment and completion through our efforts. However, when self-imposed hardships are practiced apart from Christ, they lead to behavior modification and do not produce righteousness.

When I write that hardship can be self-imposed, I mean that our faith necessitates that we are to be *crucified* with Christ. That we are to *put to death* the deeds of the body. It has become far too common to treat those exhortations as merely metaphorical. Even after you are made alive in Christ, the flesh is still waging war against your new spiritual identity. Even after you are saved and secured, you are still to take up the armor of God and fight back against the forces of darkness that threaten to attack from every side.

This is not an alarmist way of thinking; this is simply a recognition that truly pursuing Christ will require you to die to yourself *daily*. To do so means we experience a form of internal suffering, particularly to our flesh and its passions.

What could this self-imposed hardship look like?

It is denying the things that your flesh may want in light of what you know pleases God. In the name of mortifying your sin, you may decide that you will no longer keep options on your personal devices that tempt you to look lustfully at others. You may decide that you will not spend time in certain environments that trigger your flesh or that you may need to cut off ties with certain people who encourage your sinful tendencies. You may need to confess your anger, fight back against your envy, limit the opportunities for comparison, and keep your eyes down so that you do not covet that which is around you.[11]

James 1 shows us that we are all tempted and lured by our own desires, so the mortification of your sin will likely look different from mine. The goal of embracing self-imposed hardship (i.e., the process of sanctification) isn't that we would practice an identical method but an identical mission to kill sin and embrace righteousness. Romans 8:13 further shows us the necessity of this mission of mortification, as it says, "For if you live according to the flesh you will die, but if by the Spirit you put to death the deeds of the body, you will live."

The third and final form of hardship is that which is caused by association with Christ. These hardships are not simply random or externally caused because we live in a broken world. Nor are they fully internally instigated. These hardships may be called persecution. They come about because we are publicly associated with Christ and align with the words

---

11. It should be assumed that all of this activity must be spurred and sustained by the Spirit and not human striving.

of Jesus in John 15:20, "Remember the word that I said to you: 'A servant is not greater than his master.' If they persecuted me, they will also persecute you."

What does this hardship via association, this persecution, look like? For some in the global church today, should their faith be discovered, it is as serious as immediate death. But for most in the Western World, this hardship will likely result in us not fitting in with the world as smoothly or as cleanly as our flesh would desire. When we associate with Christ, we necessarily cannot live like the world, and therefore, our distinction might lead us to be ostracized or overlooked. We may lose opportunities, friendships, or even worldly credibility, all for the sake of our association with Christ. This form of hardship is not something we must chase down and demand; however, if there is no tension between you and the ways of the world, you may not be truly living out the gospel.

In outlining these three categories, you may begin to identify the ways that you recognize and relate to each. Because hardship is so varied and our sufferings so broad, each of us will have a unique context for how we face and embrace these categories. These distinctions, then, simply help us identify the means by which the enemy may try to get us to give up and lose heart.

In light of all of this, how, then, are we to endure well? How do we actually not lose heart but take heart, keeping our eyes firmly focused on the hope coming over the horizon?

Remember our original definition of endurance. It is the *faith-fueled* action of patiently and joyfully lasting or standing firm through today's hardships in view of a better tomorrow. Those words – faith-fueled – are key and are intentionally at the beginning of the definition.

You could argue that endurance without faith is impossible. Or, at the very least, it is not truly holy endurance but a form of human grit and tenacity. Faith is that integral, that central, to the work of endurance. And yet, having faith is hard, even more so in the face of hardship, because faith deals with that which is unseen.

When we face difficult circumstances, our vision, both physical and spiritual, becomes so crowded with loss, hurt, and pain that we may allow what we see to define our outlook. We can begin to see the hardship as the main story of our lives, as opposed to focusing on the unseen but unwavering truths of God, namely his grace and goodness. Though the voices surrounding us may tell us to fix our eyes on the problems at hand, Scripture consistently points us to look upward to the unseen things. In doing so, we cultivate our faith.

I think of 2 Corinthians 4:17-18, which says,

> "For this light momentary affliction is preparing for us an eternal weight of glory beyond all comparison, as we look not to the things that are seen but to the things that are unseen. For the things that are seen are transient, but the things that are unseen are eternal."

I think of Hebrews 11:1-3, which says,

> "Now faith is the assurance of things hoped for, the conviction of things not seen. For by it the people of old received their commendation. By faith we understand that the universe was created

by the word of God, so that what is seen was not made out of things that are visible."

Lastly, I think of Romans 8:24-25, which says,

> "For in this hope we were saved. Now hope that is seen is not hope. For who hopes for what he sees? But if we hope for what we do not see, we wait for it with patience."

Do you see the threads woven within these three texts? Each is powerful in its own context. But taken together, how good and glorious does the unseen grace of God appear? It is the counterweight to hardships, so much so that the Scripture calls our hardships today *light and momentary* afflictions.

This grace is the assurance of things hoped for and the conviction of our faith. It is the hope by which we were saved. What are we to do, then, in light of these promises of an unseen and future hope? Look at the end of the passage from Romans 8. We are to *wait* for it (this better, coming reality) *with patience*. Said another way, we are to endure.

When we choose the unseen over the seen, when we choose faith over what is physically in front of our faces, we are effectively prioritizing the coming reward of God's glory over the release from or the repelling of our suffering in the here and now. We are choosing to believe that the release or repelling is not the epitome of God's goodness and favor in our lives. He is working on grander, eternal scales, and when we see this, we can trust in God and his sovereignty over how we think our lives should play out today.

When it comes to externally caused hardship, it is natural to want to avoid these tensions. It is okay to pray that God would protect you, or even spare you, from these struggles.[12] When a form of external hardship comes upon you, it is encouraged to ask God to show up within the hardship. Then, you often try to address or solve the issue at hand. You absolutely can seek medical treatment for a diagnosis. You will likely report the theft to the authorities. If a storm damages your home, and you are fortunate enough to have insurance, you'll almost certainly file a claim.

The Scriptures outline various instances in which a relinquishing of suffering is requested of God. Think back on Paul's words in 2 Corinthians 12:8, when, describing the thorn in his flesh, he says, "Three times I pleaded with the Lord about this, that it should leave me." Or think of the words that Jesus himself spoke in the Garden of Gethsemane on the night before he was to be crucified, saying, "My Father, if it be possible, let this cup pass from me."[13]

However, if we come to God demanding that he remove hardships or release us from our sufferings, we miss the opportunity to hear the words Paul heard in response to his plea in 2 Corinthians 12. In the very next verse, God answers his request by saying, "My grace is sufficient for you, for my power is made perfect in weakness."

---

12. A quick note here should include that our lives are not meant to become a perpetual pursuit of dodging hardship. Of course we don't want sickness or death or devastation, but if avoiding that becomes our ultimate priority, it is an idol and it diminishes our trust in God.

13. Matthew 26:39

God wanted us to see that he is with us even amid the difficulty and darkness. That his power isn't perfected when we are at our strongest and most able. That is why in 2 Corinthians 12:10, Paul would say, "For the sake of Christ, then, I am content with weaknesses, insults, hardships, persecutions, and calamities. For when I am weak, then I am strong."

The same is true of Christ in the Garden of Gethsemane in Matthew 26. Even in his desperation, praying for an alternative path rather than embracing the terrible hardship before him,[14] Christ shows us the ultimate posture of endurance. He does pray, "My Father, if it be possible, let this cup pass from me," but he doesn't stop there, going on to also pray, "Nevertheless, not as I will, but as you will."

Do we hope that the hardship will diminish in these days? Of course. But we are not invited to demand things of God. Rather, we make our requests known to him. That implies that we are not to hinge our actions, our response, or our worship to God on whether we perceive that our hardships actually diminish.

If our prayers for the relinquishing of our hardship are not answered as we'd expect or hope, are we to blame God for being incompetent, incapable, or inconsiderate? We aren't. Should we still be committed to a posture of endurance in

---

14. Lest we are tempted to believe that Jesus didn't fully know what he was about to step into, Acts 2:23 says, "This Jesus, delivered up according to the definite plan and foreknowledge of God, you crucified and killed by the hands of lawless men." Jesus understood with complete clarity what was about to happen.

the face of what we consider to be a blatant lack of compassion? We should. We should aim, even in the tension, to stay committed to this holy work.

This is why endurance requires us to be faith-filled. We are likely to experience very real and heavy trials. Our human understanding of justice, mercy, and goodness will struggle to reconcile our experiences with the promises of an all-powerful and all-loving God. We may be tempted to feel slighted, overlooked, or even punished by this sovereign God.

And yet, we, in our limited wisdom, do not get to dictate if it is ultimately better or worse for us to remain in our present suffering. We do not get to define how or when God gets glory, whether he sustains us in our sufferings or shields us from them. We do not know, in fact, how many additional sufferings God has protected us from experiencing. We are not able, with our finite minds, to calculate the way that God turns our hardships into conduits of his grace and comfort, both for us and for those[15] whom he has assigned us to love.

---

15. This directly comes from the ideas expressed in 2 Corinthians 1:3-7, "3 Blessed be the God and Father of our Lord Jesus Christ, the Father of mercies and God of all comfort, 4 who comforts us in all our affliction, so that we may be able to comfort those who are in any affliction, with the comfort with which we ourselves are comforted by God. 5 For as we share abundantly in Christ's sufferings, so through Christ we share abundantly in comfort too. 6 If we are afflicted, it is for your comfort and salvation; and if we are comforted, it is for your comfort, which you experience when you patiently endure the same sufferings that we suffer. 7 Our hope for you is unshaken, for we know that as you share in our sufferings, you will also share in our comfort."

What we do know for sure is that the joy and glory that is to come, the better tomorrow, is so great that it is incomparable to the hardship of today. This is Romans 8:18, which says, "For I consider that the sufferings of this present time are not worth comparing with the glory that is to be revealed to us."

In faith, therefore, we should be willing to endure anything that we may "obtain the salvation that is in Christ Jesus with eternal glory."[16] There is a great day coming, sooner than we expect, and when we reach it, all the hardships and sufferings of this present world will be redeemed by the glory and goodness of God. Not erased but engulfed by a new and beautiful reality that overwhelms every ounce of our hearts with the fullness of life.

Even so, the best news for you and me today is that God is so committed to our endurance that he doesn't just prepare for us an eternal weight of glory beyond all comparison. God, in his kindness, invites us here and now to cast our troubles on him because he cares for us. He wants us to come to him in our moments of desolation and darkness, when the sky feels as if it is falling and the ground beneath our feet is opening wide.

He wants us to fall back on him, to not strive to endure in our own strength or fight our own battles, but to stand in faith. He wants us to see that he is with us in the difficulty and darkness. He was there, speaking light in the very beginning of time, and he will be there, speaking life at the end of time. He has not abandoned his children or hidden himself for the millennia in the middle.

---

16. 2 Timothy 2:10-11

God empowers us in our sufferings. He does this in many ways, but I want to point out three that seem to rise up from the Scriptures.

The first way God helps us stand firm through our hardships is by relating to us in our suffering. The writer of Hebrews says that Jesus was perfected[17] through what he suffered, thus becoming a high priest who could empathize with his people in every way. But even more than this, Romans 15:5 says, "May the God of endurance and encouragement grant you to live in such harmony with one another, in accord with Christ Jesus."

God is described as the God of endurance; it's who he is. It's also what he does. Psalm 136 is twenty-six verses long, and there are twenty-six mentions of the phrase "for his steadfast love endures forever." Why can we take comfort in the truth that God relates to us? Because he is not asking us to do something that he has not already modeled. He is the source of endurance, and therefore, when we fight to stand firm regardless of the circumstances, we are resonating with the Spirit and aligning our hearts with him.

---

17. Hebrews 2:10 - "For it was fitting that he, for whom and by whom all things exist, in bringing many sons to glory, should make the founder of their salvation perfect through suffering." This is an interesting idea because we know that Christ was at all times perfect and did not need to be "made" anything; and yet, at the same time, there was some element of his suffering and endurance that aligned with the necessary requirement of the acceptable sacrifice for sin and the redemption of mankind.

The second way God helps us stand firm and endure is by equipping us with his love. Romans 5:3-5 says,

> "Not only that, but we rejoice in our sufferings, knowing that suffering produces endurance, and endurance produces character, and character produces hope, and hope does not put us to shame, because God's love has been poured into our hearts through the Holy Spirit who has been given to us."

God does not leave those who are enduring without a source of power. Rather, he pours his love into our hearts, an action that can buoy any life threatening to sink.

Look at the progression in these verses. The fruit of our sufferings is endurance. And endurance produces character. Character goes on to reveal the fruit of hope. And why does that hope benefit our souls? Because it does not put us to shame, meaning it does not fail.

God does not come up short, but he helps us, equipping us by *"pour(ing) out his love into our hearts through the Holy Spirit."* When you know that God's love is poured out into your heart, you have a source of security to combat every insecurity. When hardship crashes against your faith, you have a deep well of love that you can draw from, a place you can return to repeatedly to remind yourself that God sees you, knows you, and loves you infinitely and intimately.

The last way that God helps us to stand firm and endure is that he chooses, in his goodness and kindness, to begin his redemptive work of restoration even now, while we are still sitting in the suffering and shadows of hardship. If we are willing to endure and embrace our hardships today in view of a greater tomorrow, then God will, today, begin to draw us towards that future horizon of glory.

Look at the words of 1 Peter 5:10, which says, "And after you have suffered a little while, the God of all grace, who has called you to his eternal glory in Christ, will himself restore, confirm, strengthen, and establish you." What a beautiful truth to celebrate and delight in! We do not know what the Lord means by "a little while." For some, that might be a few days of suffering. For others, that may be a few years of struggling. And even for others, that may mean a whole lifetime of committing to endurance.

The duration of "a little while" is not nearly as important as the reality of what comes after the "little while." After you have suffered, God himself promises to restore you. And not only that, but to also confirm you, to strengthen you, and to establish you.[18] Why? Because he is the God of all grace, and he is the one who has called you to his eternal glory in Christ; note again here the reward being the eternal weight of glory to come in Christ.[19]

God has already begun restoring you, even as you wrestle. He is confirming you, even though you may feel as if your hardships are pulling you further away from him. God is strengthening you, even in the very moments that you feel

---

18. I must be careful here to not insinuate that if our suffering passes that we will be materialistically or physically restored, confirmed, strengthened and established. Those things will all come to pass in eternity, but may not come to pass during our lives on Earth.

19. This is in line with 2 Corinthians 4:16-18 and Romans 8:18, set out earlier.

incapable and feeble. God is establishing you, even when you are feeling ill-equipped to face the hardship at hand.

We will one day praise God and worship him for the ways he wove his restoring, confirming, strengthening, and establishing power into the very fabric of our hardship, keeping us upright when everything else around us seemed to be crumbling. Praise be to God that he actively aids us in our pursuit of endurance.

If we are committed to the faith-filled action of endurance, empowered by God to stand firm and to last through today's hardships, what traits should tangibly characterize our willingness to endure? When people look at us walking through a dark moment or wrestling with a difficult circumstance, what should they see in our lives and countenance that points them to Jesus?

I think there are three words and three corresponding Scriptures that give us the roadmap for how we are to approach and embrace the practice of endurance. The words are patiently, joyfully, and expectantly.

The idea of enduring *patiently* comes from Romans 8:25: "But if we hope for what we do not see, we wait for it with patience." Why is patience such a cornerstone of endurance? Because it often takes time for us to discern how God is working, especially when we find ourselves in the middle of a season of hardship and darkness. People often use the phrase "hindsight is 20/20," yet we are tempted to think that, when it comes to seasons of hardship, we should be able to see the purpose or meaning of our suffering more fully in the present moment.

But we are not good at processing hard realities while we are in them. Thus, when we know that endurance requires patience, we are willing to embrace that we will see more clearly further down the road. That our hindsight really will be 20/20. This doesn't necessarily make it easier in the here and now, but patience helps us trust that God will prove himself faithful; we just need to endure long enough to see that faithfulness proven.

We are also to endure joyfully. I mentioned earlier that we too often view endurance as a form of resigned pessimism. We bemoan the pressure and pain of our circumstances. I am not encouraging you to force a fake cheerfulness; no one needs more disingenuity. However, look at Hebrews 10:34-36, which says,

> "For you had compassion on those in prison, and you joyfully accepted the plundering of your property, since you knew that you yourselves had a better possession and an abiding one. Therefore do not throw away your confidence, which has a great reward. For you have need of endurance, so that when you have done the will of God you may receive what is promised."

Note how those believers accepted the plundering of their property. Joyfully! Not begrudgingly or bemoaning their circumstances. They rejoiced to be plundered. Why? Follow the next verse. Because they knew that they had better possession — a greater reward! The writer even goes on to say that they needed endurance so that they might receive what was promised and what was to come. Do you see the connections here? We have a greater reward to come, one that is eternally glorious. This reward, namely Christ, instills confidence and security, so much so that we can joyfully endure the loss of all things[20] here and now.

The third and final way we are to endure is expectantly. Look at Philippians 1, particularly verses 19-21, which say,

> "Yes, and I will rejoice, for I know that through your prayers and the help of the Spirit of Jesus Christ this will turn out for my deliverance, as it is my eager expectation and hope that I will not be at all ashamed, but that with full courage now as always Christ will be honored in my body, whether by life or by death. For to me to live is Christ, and to die is gain."

When Paul wrote these words, he was in prison, in chains, for the sake of the gospel. Talk about a form of persecution and suffering, of hardship. In view of this, it is always stunning to me to see the attitude Paul has despite being in a season of heavy endurance. Is he dour? Or angry? Or bitter or forlorn? No. He is described as having an "eager expectation and hope." He was looking with joy at the better tomorrow, and in doing so, he was expectant, not only that he would presently be delivered from his imprisonment but that on that great and glorious day to come, he would eternally be

---

20. This makes me think of Paul's words in Philippians 3:7-8 when he says, "But whatever gain I had, I counted as loss for the sake of Christ. 8 Indeed, I count everything as loss because of the surpassing worth of knowing Christ Jesus my Lord. For his sake I have suffered the loss of all things and count them as rubbish, in order that I may gain Christ."

delivered from the domain of darkness and transferred into the kingdom of light.

The last words of Paul in this passage provide the key to endurance. If we are alive today, breathing in the grace of God, then we can endure with Christ. Through any and all things. But even if we are approaching death, the harshest outcome and arguably the hardest suffering, we do not need to worry or fear. For even facing death, there is gain for those who are in Christ. There is a redemption of all hardship and suffering. An embracing of the fullness of joy. There is an eternal weight of glory far beyond all comparison.

Paul closes Philippians 1 by writing in verse 29, "For it has been granted to you that for the sake of Christ you should not only believe in him but also suffer for his sake." Would we not forget that if we desire to claim the benefits of believing in Jesus, we must also be willing to claim the opportunities to suffer for his sake. This is echoed in Paul's words in Romans 8:17, which says that if we are children of God, then we are heirs, "heirs of God and fellow heirs with Christ, provided we suffer with him in order that we may also be glorified with him."

I know that staying faithful and maintaining a steady pursuit of Christ in the midst of a harrowing season may seem illogical or near impossible. But if you are looking for hope, for some shred of peace to push back against the suffering, I am confident that God has empowered you to live a faith-filled fight, to patiently, joyfully, and expectantly last by standing firm. You can make it through today's hardships in view of a better tomorrow. You have a greater inheritance to come, one that cannot be taken or tarnished. So, keep pressing on and keep pressing in. You are closer to eternity's glory than you know.

In the struggling with you,

J. Daghe

1.

Which form of hardship is most present in your life right now, and which is most lacking? What are a few practical ways that you can both take heart for the trials ahead and not lose heart for the trials you may be in right now?

I noted three words for how we are to embrace the practice of endurance: patiently, joyfully, and expectantly. Which of these three is most challenging to you, and why? What would it look like to grow in that characteristic in the midst of your trials?

Lord, you are the source of endurance, and you know what it means to stand fast under trial and tribulation. Teach me again, Lord, to turn to you no matter my circumstance, that I could find refuge in your strength, joy in your example, and peace in your power.

Acknowledgements

The older I get and the more I read, the more I tend to appreciate these last few pages of a book. These pages are not merely filler or fodder to appease a particular group of people. These might be among the most vulnerable and authentic pages in any book, because anyone who has set out to write anything knows that it is virtually impossible in a vacuum. Not only do all writers, by and large, require readers (or else the writing is, in many ways, incomplete), but they also require support and a team of people who help in countless ways. Author Diana Pavlac Glyer, in her book *Bandersnatch*, would use the word "resonator," which I have grown quite fond of.

So, without much more ado or philosophy, here are many of the small army of resonators who helped fuel this content and encouraged this project to reach completion.

To Lindsey, I am grateful that you not only entertain but also actively listen to my repetitive ramblings of these ideas and Scriptures. Anyone married to a writer knows that you are signed up to be some combination of sounding board, negotiator, and cheerleader, but there is a way to just do the work or to embrace it, and you have embraced it, my dear. I am forever humbled by and thankful for your belief in me, and I love you, 3000.

To my parents, Bret and Laura, and my sister, JoJo – thank you for your constant encouragement and support. To Clayton De Fur, I cherish our conversations. To Alex Prichodko, your push of encouragement that morning at breakfast was exactly what I needed. To Kaylie, Craig, and Delores, there are few things better than marrying into a wonderful family, and I constantly thank God that I get to belong to yours.

To Wayne, Alpha, Epsi, and Ray — my friends and fellow brothers in Christ whose hearts and hunger for God have shaped me more than nearly anything else on this side of eternity: thank you. It is among the rarest treasures to find one, let alone four, brothers who genuinely love the Lord with all the wisdom in their heads and all the marrow in their bones. Press on, dear friends, for we are closer to home today than ever before.

To my mentors and friends in Atlanta, with whom I've had countless conversations over the years, and who have walked with me as I've attempted to grow up into Christ: your encouragement and edification have molded me into the man, husband, father, and writer I am today. There are too many to name them all, but special thanks to Luke Baker, Kristine Jahnke, Ray Coury, Kevin Marks, James Vore,

Jake Gross, Bryson Vogeltanz, Jason Dyba, Matthew Marshall, Jon Tsang, Jon Woodson, Caleb Hurb, Matthew Samuels, and Venu Devarapalli.

This content would never have made it from my Word document to a beautifully designed book without the talented and triumphant work of my friend and designer, Katie Watford. Katie, your heart for matching holy content with beautiful art is a window into the kind of baptized imagination I think will be true of us in eternity. Thank you for your gift and grace.

This book would not be possible without dozens of supporters who financially backed its production and publication. To those who supported this collection on Kickstarter, I am forever grateful for your kind and gracious support. Your generosity went far beyond a donation; you helped reinforce my belief that this content was both beneficial and necessary. A full list of supporters is available on the following page.

Finally, I want to acknowledge you, the reader. I may or may not personally know you, but regardless, if you have made it this far, I am inspired by your desire to grow up into maturity in Christ. I am praying right now as I type these words for your continued growth and conformity into his image, that the eyes of your heart would be more enlightened here and now than they were before you first read these essays. That God, through his Spirit, would strengthen your faith, establishing it within his good and glorious foundation of love, and that he himself would restore and redeem you, confirming his work in you as he brings it to completion at the day of Christ.

That day is coming, and I pray that we meet it with wonder, awe, and holy fear for our God is a consuming fire. What a delight it is to be consumed by him.

Sub specie aeternitatis,

Jake

KICKSTARTER SUPPORTERS:

Jason Dyba

Jon & Jordan Woodson

Emma Bradley

Bryson Vogeltanz

Alex Hunter

Hannah & Jeremy Vincent

Corey Ebert

Kristine Jahnke

Chandler Saunders

Janelle Nobles

Crystal Mitchell

Davis & Grace Brown

Michele Wlodarek

Lindsay Guerin

Clayton & JoJo De Fur

Bret & Laura Daghe

Luke & Sarah Baker

Emily Buchanan

Sara Palmisano

Caleb & Courtney Hurd

John Ragland Jr

Ian Agnew

Allie Coleman Techmanski

Matthew Marshall

Sam Moran

Britt Adams

Seth & Nicole Fischer

Campbell Sims

Addison Bradford

Mike Killian

Erika Foxworth

Craig & Delores Waltz

Hoke Bryan

Jeff & Jourdan Johnson

Adam & Petra Hunkler

Will Severns

Kevin & Susan Marks

Jonathan Pickens

Lauren Brands

Michael Craig

Andi Shen

Mark Caswell

Seth Glasscock

Adrienne Kelly

Eric & Abby Hunkler

Bennett Tatgenhorst

Kaylie & Alex Prichodko

Jeffrey Johnson

Alex Campbell

Sundar Shivraj

John & Tina Campell

Jon Tsang

Leighton Ching

Wes Williams

Larry & Dawn Daghe

Dan & Gayle Cole

Jake Daghe is a writer, thinker, and lifelong learner. He is the Content Director and Editor for Passion Publishing, an imprint partner with HarperCollins Christian Publishing. He has a Master's of Christian Leadership from Dallas Theological Seminary and teaches theology classes at Passion City Church. He also consults with churches on discipleship and formation ministries.

This collection features Jake's first published books and spotlights his heart for enriching theology and spiritual formation.

Jake lives in Westfield, Indiana, with his wife, Lindsey, and their three daughters. He enjoys board games, hand-written notes, popcorn, and visiting national parks with his family.

For more details or to contact Jake, visit jakedaghe.com.